Contents

Pineapple Table Runner & Coaster Set

Size: **Table Runner:** 31¾ inches L x 10⅝ inches D
(80.6cm x 27cm)
Coaster: 5¼ inches W x 5¼ inches D
(13.3cm x 13.3cm)
Coaster Holder: 5½ inches W x 1⅝ inches H x
5½ inches D (14cm x 4.1cm x 14cm)
Skill Level: Intermediate

Materials

❑ 4½ sheets 7-count plastic canvas
❑ Uniek Needloft plastic canvas yarn as listed
   in color key
❑ #16 tapestry needle
❑ Hand-sewing needle and golden brown thread

Stitching Step by Step

1 Cut plastic canvas according to graphs (pages 3–6). Cut one 36-hole x 36-hole piece for holder base. Base will remain unstitched.

2 Stitch pieces following graphs, filling in around motifs on panel pieces and coasters following yellow Slanted Gobelin Stitch pattern.

3 Using maple through step 4, Overcast coaster. Whipstitch holder sides together, and then Whipstitch sides to unstitched base; Overcast top edges.

4 Overcast table runner panels. Stitch end panels to center panel with hand-sewing needle and golden brown thread.

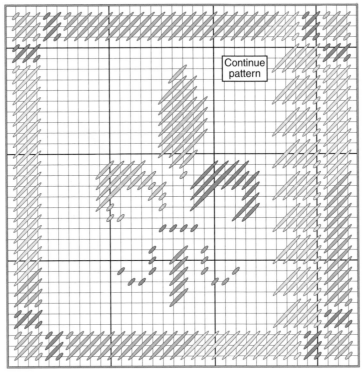

Continue pattern

Coaster
34 holes x 34 holes
Cut 4

COLOR KEY	
Yards	**Plastic Canvas Yarn**
40 (36.6m)	■ Rust #09
35 (32m)	☐ Pumpkin #12
80 (73.2m)	■ Maple #13
35 (32m)	☐ Fern #23
25 (22.9m)	☐ Mermaid #53
150 (137.2m)	☐ Yellow #57
30 (27.5m)	☐ Bright green #61
Color numbers given are for Uniek Needloft plastic canvas yarn.	

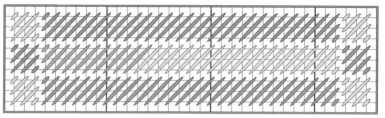

Coaster Holder Side A
36 holes x 10 holes
Cut 1

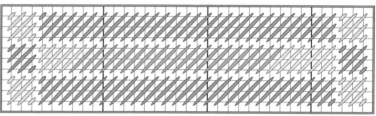

Coaster Holder Side B
36 holes x 10 holes
Cut 1

COLOR KEY

Yards	Plastic Canvas Yarn
40 (36.6m)	■ Rust #09
35 (32m)	□ Pumpkin #12
80 (73.2m)	■ Maple #13
35 (32m)	■ Fern #23
25 (22.9m)	■ Mermaid #53
150 (137.2m)	□ Yellow #57
30 (27.5m)	□ Bright green #61

Color numbers given are for Uniek
Needloft plastic canvas yarn.

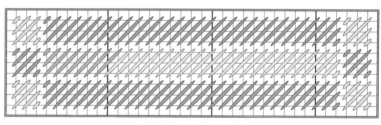

Coaster Holder Side C
36 holes x 10 holes
Cut 1

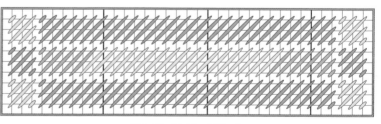

Coaster Holder Side D
36 holes x 10 holes
Cut 1

Continue pattern

Center Panel
70 holes x 70 holes
Cut 1

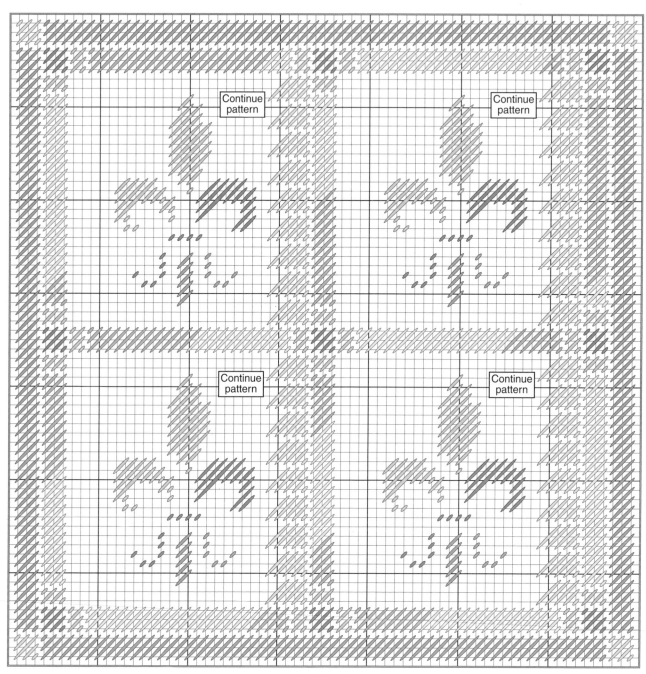

End Panel
70 holes x 70 holes
Cut 2

COLOR KEY

Yards	Plastic Canvas Yarn
40 (36.6m)	■ Rust #09
35 (32m)	□ Pumpkin #12
80 (73.2m)	■ Maple #13
35 (32m)	■ Fern #23
25 (22.9m)	□ Mermaid #53
150 (137.2m)	□ Yellow #57
30 (27.5m)	□ Bright green #61

Color numbers given are for Uniek
Needloft plastic canvas yarn.

Lace Table Runner & Coaster Set

Size: **Table Runner:** 28 inches L x 10⅜ inches D
(71.1cm x 26.4cm)
Coaster: 4¾ inches W x 4¾ inches D
(12.1cm x 12.1cm)
Coaster Holder: 5½ inches W x 1¾ inches H x
5½ inches D (14cm x 4.4cm x 14cm)
Skill Level: Intermediate

Materials

❑ 4½ sheets 7-count plastic canvas
❑ Red Heart Super Saver Art. E300 medium weight
yarn as listed in color key
❑ Uniek Needloft plastic canvas yarn as listed
in color key
❑ Uniek Needloft iridescent craft cord as listed
in color key
❑ ⅛-inch/3mm-wide white ribbon
❑ #16 tapestry needle
❑ Hand-sewing needle and white thread

Stitching Step by Step

1 Cut plastic canvas according to graphs (pages 8–11).
Cut one 36-hole x 36-hole piece for holder base.
Base will remain unstitched.

2 Stitch pieces following graphs, working Continental Stitches in uncoded areas as follows: white background with white iridescent craft cord, peach background with white medium weight yarn.

3 Overcast coasters with gray. Whipstitch holder sides together with white medium weight yarn and white iridescent craft cord. Using white medium weight yarn, Whipstitch sides to unstitched base; Overcast top edges.

4 Insert ribbon through hole indicated at one blue dot on one holder side. Weave ribbon with a Running Stitch, working around all four sides following graph; bring ribbon out through remaining hole with blue dot. Tie ends together in a bow; trim ends. If desired, tack bow in place with hand-sewing needle and white thread.

5 Overcast table runner panels with white medium weight yarn and white iridescent craft cord. Stitch panels together with hand-sewing needle and white thread.

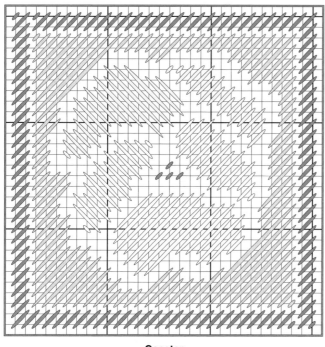

Coaster
31 holes x 31 holes
Cut 4

COLOR KEY

Yards	Medium Weight Yarn
70 (64m)	☐ White #311
35 (32m)	☐ Soft white #316
	Uncoded areas on peach background are white #311 Continental Stitches
	Plastic Canvas Yarn
30 (27.5m)	☐ Silver #37
40 (36.6m)	■ Gray #38
80 (73.2m)	☐ White #41
	Iridescent Craft Cord
30 (27.5m)	Uncoded areas on white background are white #55033 Continental Stitches
	⁄ White #55033 Overcast and Whipstitch
	⅛-Inch (3mm) Ribbon
1 (1m)	▬ White Running Stitch

Color numbers given are for Red Heart Super Saver Art. E300 medium weight yarn and Uniek Needloft plastic canvas yarn and iridescent craft cord.

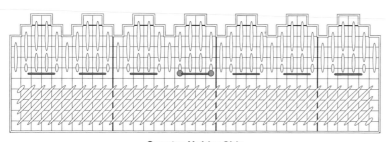

Coaster Holder Side
36 holes x 11 holes
Cut 4

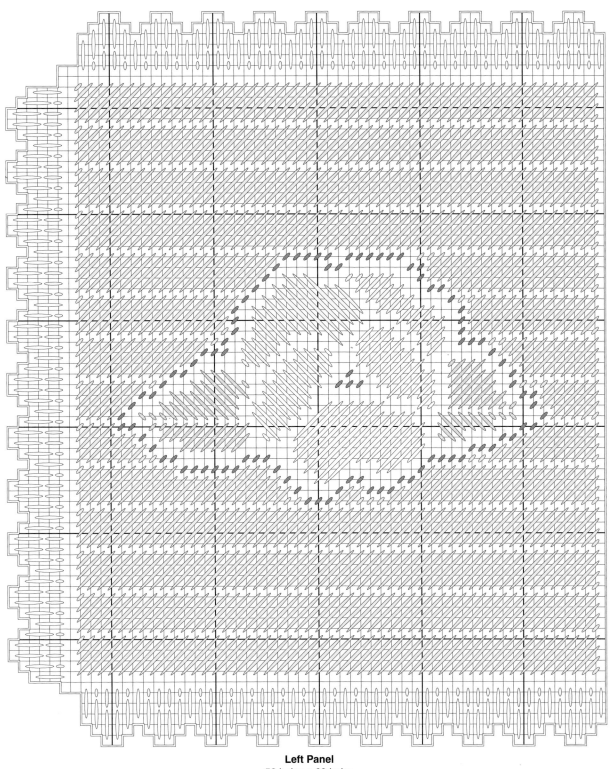

Left Panel
58 holes x 69 holes
Cut 1

Center Panel
68 holes x 69 holes
Cut 1

COLOR KEY

Yards	Medium Weight Yarn
70 (64m)	☐ White #311
35 (32m)	☐ Soft white #316
	Uncoded areas on peach background are white #311 Continental Stitches

Plastic Canvas Yarn

Yards	
30 (27.5m)	☐ Silver #37
40 (36.6m)	■ Gray #38
80 (73.2m)	☐ White #41

Iridescent Craft Cord

Yards	
30 (27.5m)	Uncoded areas on white background are white #55033 Continental Stitches
	⁄ White #55033 Overcast and Whipstitch

⅛-Inch (3mm) Ribbon

Yards	
1 (1m)	▬ White Running Stitch

Color numbers given are for Red Heart Super Saver Art. E300 medium weight yarn and Uniek Needloft plastic canvas yarn and iridescent craft cord.

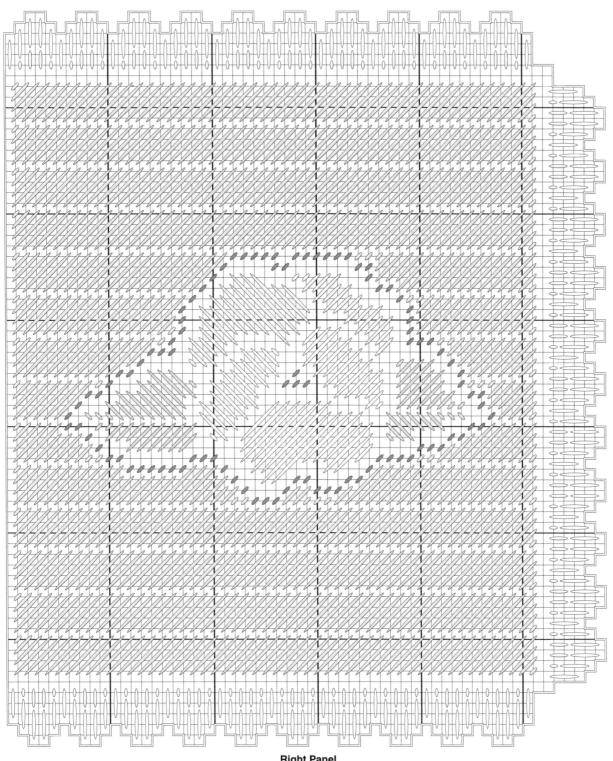

Right Panel
58 holes x 69 holes
Cut 1

Tile Table Runner & Coaster Set

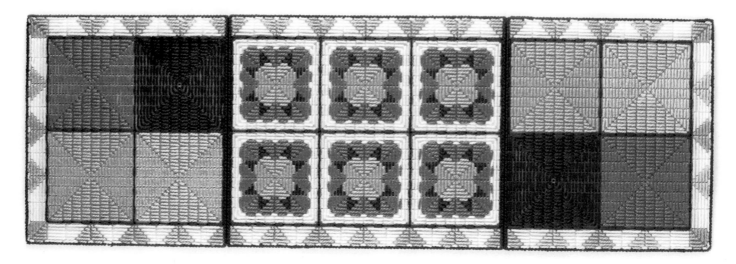

Size: **Table Runner:** 32 inches L x 10⅜ inches D
(81.3cm x 26.4cm)
Coaster: 4½ inches W x 4½ inches D
(11.4cm x 11.4cm)
Coaster Holder: 5 inches W x 1⅛ inches H x
5 inches D (12.7cm x 2.9cm x 12.7cm)
Skill Level: Intermediate

Materials

❑ 4½ sheets 7-count plastic canvas
❑ Uniek Needloft plastic canvas yarn as listed
in color key
❑ #16 tapestry needle
❑ Hand-sewing needle and navy thread

Stitching Step by Step

1 Cut plastic canvas according to graphs (pages 13–16). Cut one 32-hole x 32-hole piece for holder base. Base will remain unstitched.

2 Stitch pieces following graphs.

3 Using dark royal throughout, Overcast coasters. Whipstitch holder sides together, and then Whipstitch holder sides to unstitched base; Overcast top edges. Overcast table runner panels.

4 Stitch panels together with hand-sewing needle and navy thread.

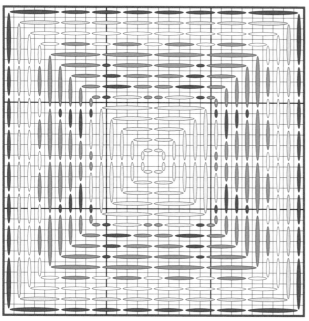

Coaster
29 holes x 29 holes
Cut 4

COLOR KEY

Yards	Plastic Canvas Yarn
65 (59.5m)	▨ Royal #32
35 (32m)	☐ Sail blue #35
39 (35.7m)	▨ Silver #37
45 (41.2m)	☐ White #41
85 (77.8m)	■ Dark royal #48
55 (50.3m)	☐ Bright blue #60

Color numbers given are for Uniek
Needloft plastic canvas yarn.

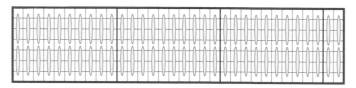

Coaster Holder Side
32 holes x 7 holes
Cut 4
Stitch 1 as graphed,
Stitch 1 each, replacing
bright blue with royal,
sail blue and dark royal

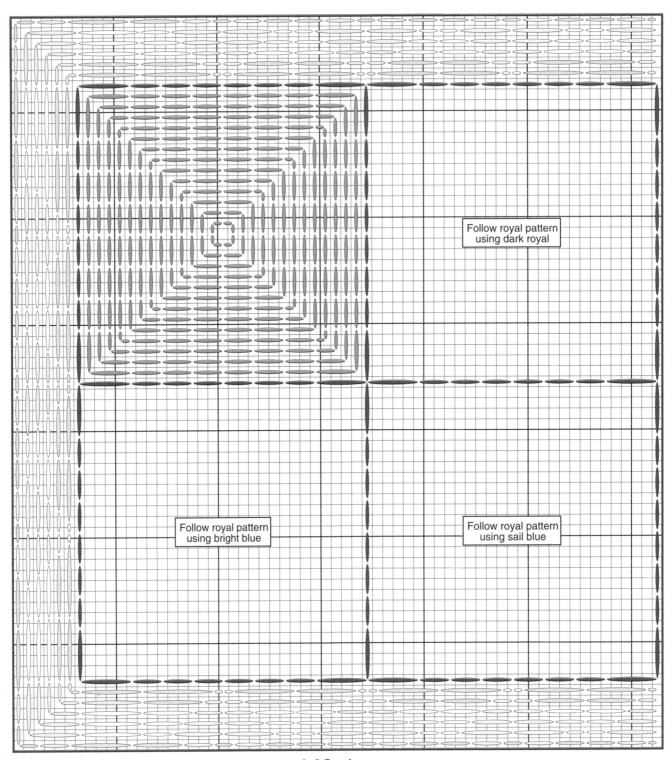

Left Panel
63 holes x 69 holes
Cut 1

Follow royal pattern
using dark royal

Follow royal pattern
using bright blue

Follow royal pattern
using sail blue

COLOR KEY

Yards		Plastic Canvas Yarn
65 (59.5m)	▨	Royal #32
35 (32m)	☐	Sail blue #35
39 (35.7m)	☐	Silver #37
45 (41.2m)	☐	White #41
85 (77.8m)	■	Dark royal #48
55 (50.3m)	☐	Bright blue #60

Color numbers given are for Uniek
Needloft plastic canvas yarn.

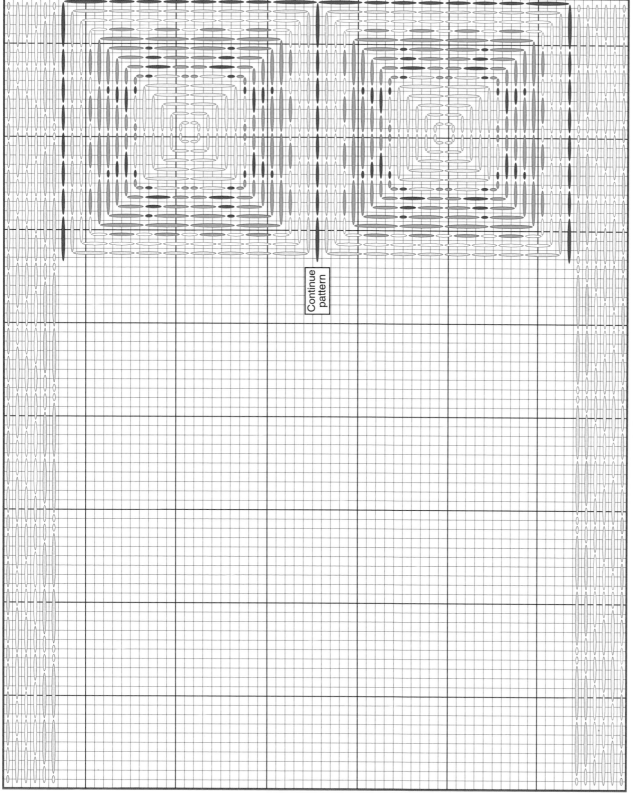

Continue pattern

Center Panel
85 holes x 69 holes
Cut 1

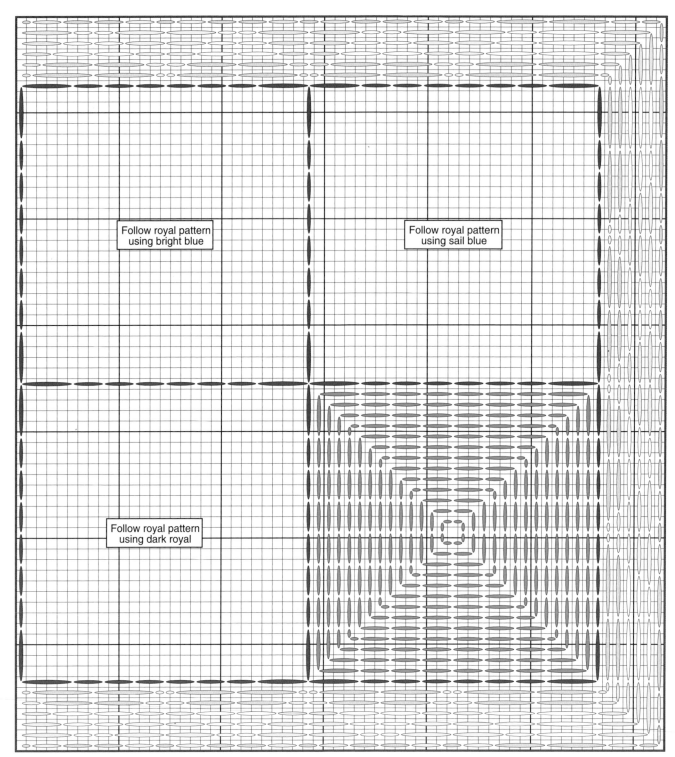

Follow royal pattern
using bright blue

Follow royal pattern
using sail blue

Follow royal pattern
using dark royal

Right Panel
63 holes x 69 holes
Cut 1

COLOR KEY

Yards	Plastic Canvas Yarn
65 (59.5m)	■ Royal #32
35 (32m)	□ Sail blue #35
39 (35.7m)	▨ Silver #37
45 (41.2m)	□ White #41
85 (77.8m)	■ Dark royal #48
55 (50.3m)	□ Bright blue #60

Color numbers given are for Uniek
Needloft plastic canvas yarn.

Fruit Table Runner & Coaster Set

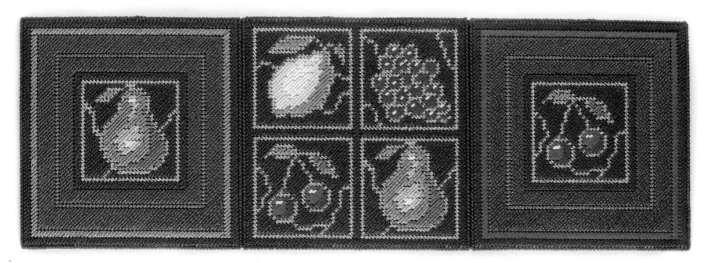

Size: **Table Runner:** 27½ inches L x 9¼ inches D
(69.9cm x 23.5cm)
Coaster: 4⅞ inches W x 4⅞ inches D
(12.4cm x 12.4cm)
Coaster Holder: 5⅝ inches W x
1½ inches H x 5⅝ inches D (14.3cm x
3.8cm x 14.3cm)
Skill Level: Intermediate

Materials

❏ 4½ sheets 7-count plastic canvas
❏ Uniek Needloft plastic canvas yarn as listed
in color key
❏ Uniek Needloft metallic craft cord as listed
in color key
❏ #16 tapestry needle
❏ Hand-sewing needle and brown thread

Stitching Step by Step

1 Cut plastic canvas according to graphs (pages
18–23). Cut one 36-hole x 36-hole piece for holder
base. Base will remain unstitched.

2 Stitch pieces following graphs, working uncoded
areas with gold metallic craft cord Continental
Stitches.

3 Overcast grapes coaster with purple, lemon coaster
with gold, cherries coaster with burgundy, and pear
coaster with holly.

4 Using brown throughout, Whipstitch holder sides together, and then Whipstitch holder sides to unstitched base; Overcast top edges. Overcast table runner panels.

5 Stitch panels together with hand-sewing needle and brown thread.

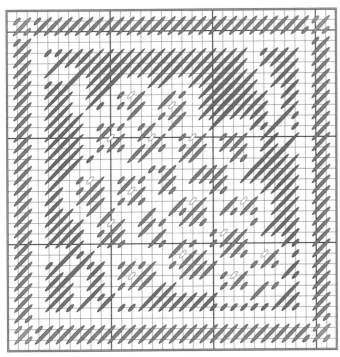

Grapes Coaster
32 holes x 32 holes
Cut 1

Cherries Coaster
32 holes x 32 holes
Cut 1

COLOR KEY	
Yards	**Plastic Canvas Yarn**
21 (19.3m)	Red #01
8 (7.4m)	Burgundy #03
45 (41.2m)	Cinnamon #14
120 (110m)	Brown #15
9 (8.3m)	Gold #17
3 (2.8m)	Lemon #20
5 (4.6m)	Fern #23
20 (18.3m)	Holly #27
25 (22.9m)	Christmas green #28
2 (1.9m)	Eggshell #39
5 (4.6m)	Purple #46
12 (11m)	Yellow #57
11 (10.1m)	Bright purple #64
	Metallic Craft Cord
40 (36.6m)	Uncoded areas are gold #55501 Continental Stitches
Color numbers given are for Uniek Needloft plastic canvas yarn and metallic craft cord.	

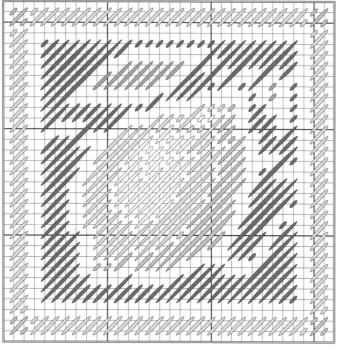

Lemon Coaster
32 holes x 32 holes
Cut 1

Pear Coaster
32 holes x 32 holes
Cut 1

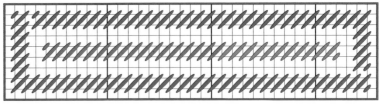

Coaster Holder Side A
36 holes x 9 holes
Cut 1

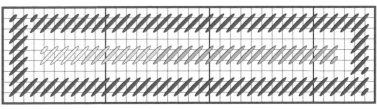

Coaster Holder Side B
36 holes x 9 holes
Cut 1

COLOR KEY

Yards	Plastic Canvas Yarn
21 (19.3m)	■ Red #01
8 (7.4m)	■ Burgundy #03
45 (41.2m)	■ Cinnamon #14
120 (110m)	■ Brown #15
9 (8.3m)	■ Gold #17
3 (2.8m)	☐ Lemon #20
5 (4.6m)	☐ Fern #23
20 (18.3m)	■ Holly #27
25 (22.9m)	■ Christmas green #28
2 (1.9m)	☐ Eggshell #39
5 (4.6m)	■ Purple #46
12 (11m)	☐ Yellow #57
11 (10.1m)	■ Bright purple #64
	Metallic Craft Cord
40 (36.6m)	Uncoded areas are gold #55501 Continental Stitches

Color numbers given are for Uniek Needloft plastic canvas yarn and metallic craft cord.

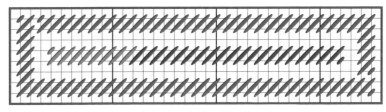

Coaster Holder Side C
36 holes x 9 holes
Cut 1

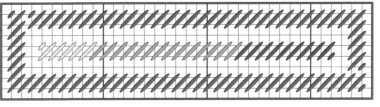

Coaster Holder Side D
36 holes x 9 holes
Cut 1

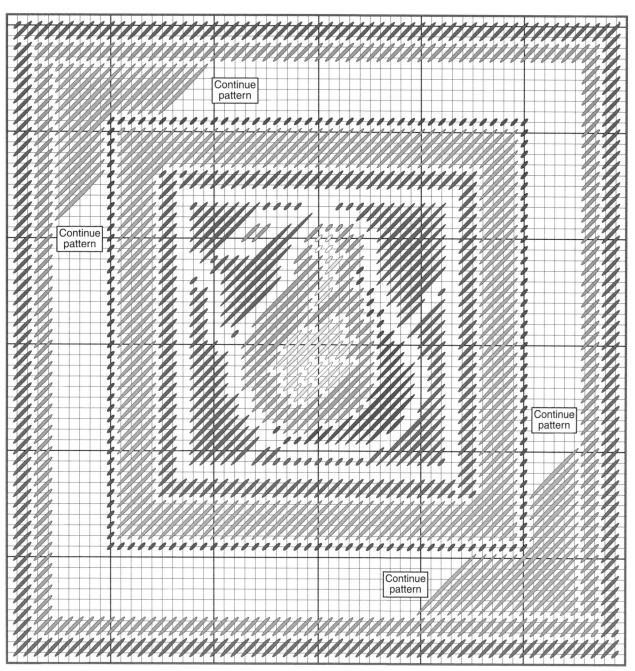

Left Panel
60 holes x 61 holes
Cut 1

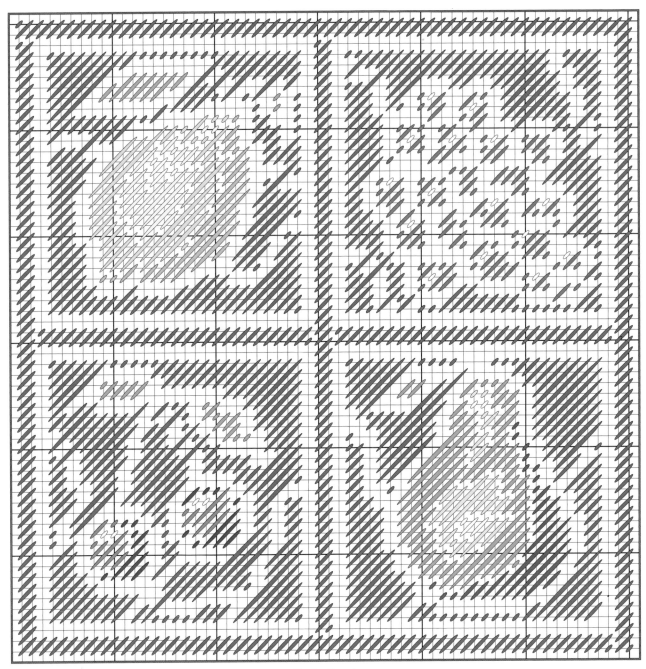

Center Panel
61 holes x 61 holes
Cut 1

COLOR KEY	
Yards	**Plastic Canvas Yarn**
21 (19.3m)	Red #01
8 (7.4m)	Burgundy #03
45 (41.2m)	Cinnamon #14
120 (110m)	Brown #15
9 (8.3m)	Gold #17
3 (2.8m)	Lemon #20
5 (4.6m)	Fern #23
20 (18.3m)	Holly #27
25 (22.9m)	Christmas green #28
2 (1.9m)	Eggshell #39
5 (4.6m)	Purple #46
12 (11m)	Yellow #57
11 (10.1m)	Bright purple #64
Metallic Craft Cord	
40 (36.6m)	Uncoded areas are gold #55501 Continental Stitches

Color numbers given are for Uniek Needloft plastic canvas yarn and metallic craft cord.

Right Panel
60 holes x 61 holes
Cut 1

Annie's Attic®

Table Runners & More is published by DRG, 306 East Parr Road, Berne, IN 46711. Printed in USA. Copyright © 2010 DRG. All rights reserved. This publication may not be reproduced in part or in whole without written permission from the publisher.

RETAIL STORES: If you would like to carry this pattern book or any other DRG publications, visit DRGwholesale.com

Every effort has been made to ensure that the instructions in this publication are complete and accurate. We cannot, however, take responsibility for human error, typographical mistakes or variations in individual work. Please visit AnniesCustomerCare.com to check for pattern updates.

ISBN: 978-1-59635-331-2

Printed in USA

1 2 3 4 5 6 7 8 9

Shopping for Supplies

For supplies, first shop your local craft and needlework stores. Some supplies may be found in fabric, hardware and discount stores. If you are unable to find the supplies you need, please visit anniesattic.com.

Getting Started

Before You Cut

Buy one brand of canvas for each entire project as brands can differ slightly in the distance between bars. Count holes carefully from the graph before you cut, using the bolder lines that show each 10 holes. These 10-count lines begin from the left side for vertical lines and from the bottom for horizontal lines. Mark canvas before cutting; then remove all marks completely before stitching. If the piece is cut in a rectangular or square shape and is either not worked, or worked with only one color and one type of stitch, the graph is not included in the pattern. Instead, the cutting and stitching instructions are given in the general instructions or with the individual project instructions.

Covering the Canvas

Bring needle up from back of work, leaving a short length of yarn on back of canvas; work over short length to secure. To end a thread, weave needle and thread through the wrong side of your last few stitches; clip. Follow the numbers on the small graphs beside each stitch illustration; bring your needle up from the back of the work on odd numbers and down through the front of the work on even numbers. Work embroidery stitches last, after the canvas has been completely covered by the needlepoint stitches.

Basic Stitches

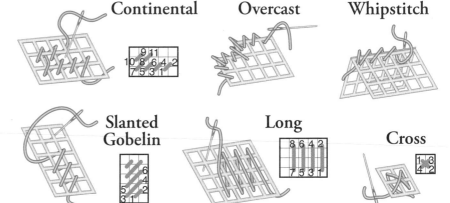

Embroidery Stitches

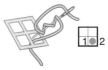
French Knot

Lazy Daisy

Backstitch

Straight

METRIC KEY:
millimeters = (mm)
centimeters = (cm)
meters = (m)
grams = (g)